From Hand To Mouth

Jenny Collins

From Hand To Mouth

Copyright © collinz creation
February 2004

All Rights reserved
No part of this book may be reproduced in any form by photocopying or by electronic means, including information, storage or retrieval systems, without permission in writing from both the copyright owner and the publisher of this book.

ISBN 0-9547113-0-0

First Edition 2004
Published by
Workers' Health Advice Team
2nd Floor, Auburn House
Upper Piccadilly
Bradford
BD1 3NU

Acknowledgements

To Barry for the artwork, Jane for finalising, Roy for the title, and Bridget for thoughts.
I express my sincere gratitude and appreciation for all the help and support I have been given over the last 9 years and I particularly want to thank all those to whom I dedicate this book.

For LOVE & SUPPORT in Adversity

I dedicate this book to:

My wonderful husband, Barry (my grammar man!) who embraces the brunt of my experience; my beautiful children, Paul, Wendy & Nicky just for being them, and who had to grow up so very, very fast; my family - Linda, Paul, Rebecca & Dominic who helped bring joy and laughter back into my life, mums, Phil, Chris, Sandy and Liz for being there; my very dear friends - Carol my 'SS' and bag carrier - it wasn't easy for you, I know; Anne my 'VSF' for the gift of laughter, for knowing just when to lift me to heights of infectious giggles; Lesley for her valiant efforts above and beyond the call of friendship during the harrowing days of my grievance; Carol my confidant and now work colleague and friend; Jean, such a lovely, warm gentle soul; Christine for giving me hope and the determination to persevere; Kay for showing me how to hug; Bridget & Roy for their inspiration; Karen & Cynthia for all their hard work; Dr Khan for not giving up on me; Professor Bird for accepting my referral; Brian for reflexology; Yoshiko for acupuncture; Liz for aromatherapy massages; Nick for PC help; Sonia for surrounding me in positivity; Grace, a truly amazing lady who inspires me to embrace life; Helen for the magical experience of Jessica's birth; Linda & Carol for helping to 'turn the knobs'; Wapping friends; my Australian 'Guys'; Louise L. Hay; Sheila and colleagues for their understanding; WHAT & BOHP colleagues, Hilary, Karan, Cath, Mike, Neville, Martin, George, Jane for stepping in at the last minute!; Carolyn, Judith, Jane; Sonja & Richard; Penny & Team; Bradford Repetitive Strain Injury support group members; All who have believed in me ....

THANK YOU

XXXX

From Hand To Mouth

Copyright © collinz creation
February 2004
by Jenny Collins

The author is grateful for permission to include details about WHAT, VoicePower and Shipley College, and for the kind permission of Professor Buckle for the use of his information.

CONTENTS

	Page
Introduction	9
Life -	
Personal	11
Medical	20
Financial	23
Professional	24
Support Group	26
My Life Now	28
Future	32
Conclusion	37
Contacts	38

Introduction

I always wanted to learn to type. At the age of 30 I went back to school and learnt how. I loved it! Being diagnosed with tenosynovitis in 1995, 6 years later, was devastating. Tenosynovitis is a repetitive strain injury (RSI). A repetitive strain injury is not necessarily in the upper limbs. For example, the feet or knees may be affected. A repetitive strain injury is caused when a task requires small, rapid, repeated movements, often whilst maintaining a static posture, in my case caused in the work place due to the bad ergonomic set-up of the office: heating, lighting, space, furniture and lack of certain items of equipment and training. Finding out that my injury was work-related due to the illegal set-up of my visual display unit (VDU) workstation was just as devastating and, unbelievable - it could have been prevented!

All I had done was to work hard and yet, because health and safety regulations had been ignored, I had developed an injury that was taking over my life. The effect of this injury also encroached on my family and friends and it felt quite catastrophic at times.

Tenosynovitis affects one's manual dexterity, grip and fine mobility functions. As both my upper limbs are affected my diagnosis is bilateral tenosynovitis.

Life

Personal

On a morning, on waking, my hands and wrists are often heavy and stiff. Around the inner wrists there is often throbbing pain. Sometimes my right elbow and my neck are affected with symptoms. Symptoms range from hot, burning twangs to shooting pains in the fingers, pains up the forearms as if a knitting needle were stuck in there, pins and needles, cold and a numbing sensation. The colder weather aggravates my symptoms. There were times in the early stages of my injury where I would have quite gladly let someone chop off both my hands and arms.

About an hour or so after waking, showering and dressing, my hands and wrists will, on most days now, have loosened up. Sometimes there will be twinges of pain in the wrists and round the thumbs and fingers, sometimes on the back of my hands. Sometimes swelling, pins and needles and/or tingling sensations. As I go through the day certain activities will trigger swelling around the base of the index and middle fingers and around the thumb area. Some days I will have bouts of shooting pains in my wrists. My fingers have also been known to 'lock' on me from time to time.

In the early stages of my tenosynovitis, for about 4/5 years, these symptoms were excruciatingly painful in my every day life. Nowadays I push myself to the limit, knowing what I can reasonably do, and on days when my mind is very, very active and wishes my body to be so too, pushing myself to the limit results in a flare-up that lasts anything from an hour to weeks. There are days when you just do not want to be dependent upon people all the time so "bloody mindedness" takes over. The mental feeling of accomplishment is often worth the pain of a flare-up!

Over the last eighteen months I have had about 9 flare ups, though one of these flare ups did last for 3 weeks.

All of the following are things that are taken for granted by most people - no longer by me. There are things I just do not attempt. Like pushing the trolley around the supermarket, carrying heavy jars, bottles and tins, loading the shopping in and out of the car, carrying the shopping bags from the car to the house. Washing the car, filling it with petrol, lifting open the bonnet, using the air pressure gauge, changing a tyre (something I have done in the past), opening the door of the petrol station. D.I.Y. Using shears to trim back bushes in the garden or weeding. Putting out the wheelie bin. Pegging washing out on the line. Carrying an umbrella, because of the need to sustain the grip and maintain the height at which the arm is raised in holding the umbrella. Chopping and peeling vegetables, whisking, beating, mashing, draining hot liquids and baking.

Keeping the family home clean was impossible in the early stages of my tenosynovitis. Many a day I have sat in tears staring at the dust. Things such as hoovering, dusting, cleaning windows, shampooing carpets, etc all require the gripping action. I do ironing in small manageable amounts these days.

There are things for which I need another person's support. When travelling on public transport I need somebody with me so that they can get up at the correct stop for me. Then when the vehicle has actually stopped I can stand-up and alight without having to hold on and have the jerk of braking jar through my wrists. When going on long walks a bum bag is manageable but it is also advisable to carry a packed lunch, water bottle and first aid kit. Even a backpack adds extra pressure across my shoulders so again a support person is needed. At Christmas time, when shopping for gifts I need the support of an extra person to carry the bags.

There are days when I find it extremely frustrating when out and about. Lots of shops and offices have such heavy doors that they are sometimes almost impossible to open. I will use both hands to prise open the door a couple of inches and then stick my knee into the door using force from my leg to open the door. Just having to prise open a door a couple of inches can often make me wince with pain, as jarring of the wrists will often happen.

I will also forget on occasions when I go into supermarkets that I cannot carry more than two or three items and I end up with about five or six, albeit small things, in my hand, wishing I'd never decided to pick up so many things. I then usually find myself fumbling with my change!

I do not exert the same pressure now when cleaning my teeth as I did prior to having tenosynovitis so I now require regular de-scaling at the dentist.

I had long hair since the age of 13 and at the time of my diagnosis it was also permed. My hair became increasingly difficult to manage and extremely reluctantly I had to have my hair cut shorter. I now keep my hair no longer than shoulder length and have to have regular haircuts. I would love to go back to having long, curly hair.

I am not a person who wears make up every day, but I do like to put on make up if I am going to a 'do'. The intricate movements required in putting on make up cause pain so I use the bare minimum. I choose clothes that do not have fiddly buttons and require a minimum of ironing. I look around for slip on shoes or boots with a zip so as not to fiddle with laces, although I do have to tie laces as my role as swimming teacher requires me to wear trainers. (Recently I found a pair of slip on trainers, which are fashionable - what a bonus!) On the odd occasion when I see an item of clothing that I really like, but that would be difficult for me to fasten, I may allow my "bloody mindedness" to kick in and would then have to ask the help of a family member when I want to wear the item. Most days, even the early hours of the long hot summer days, I wear gloves. Letting my hands get too cold causes them to go numb and stops them functioning altogether.

Some social activities are difficult. Going for a drink in a busy pub involves me either having to be near a table on which to place my drink or asking whoever I am with to hold my drink for me. As an avid letter writer I reverted to telephoning friends, using a phone with a headset.

Family activities with my three children, such as bowling, cycling, ice-skating and ball games, became spectator sports for me. When I was diagnosed with tenosynovitis, back in February 1995, my children were still relatively young, being aged 13, 12 and 10 respectively. It was very difficult for them to understand the magnitude of what was happening to their mum.

One of the hardest things to endure whilst living with tenosynovitis has been mentally accepting my condition. I have a physical disability. Having to ask for help means a loss of independence. Sometimes help cannot be forthcoming for whatever reason and therefore you have to accept the fact that what you would like to happen just isn't going to.

Life

Medical

Numerous visits to people in the medical profession followed my tenosynovitis diagnosis. I was fortunate in having not only a doctor but also an Occupational Health worker at my surgery who both strongly believe in work place injuries. I was advised immediately that work was the cause of my repetitive strain injury.

Having previously only been on sick leave for 1 week (when I was 19 years old) I found this period of time in my life extremely difficult.

Nobody in the medical profession has been willing to put a timescale on when this injury will get better. 'Could be ten years' they might say.

Five years down the line I managed to get a referral to a Professor in rheumatology whose help has been invaluable. I received the correct adverse neural tension (ANT) physiotherapy and found that what I had been doing myself to treat my tenosynovitis through trial and error over the previous 5 years, was, in actual fact their procedure. I have since been able to incorporate my physiotherapy exercises into my toning table exercise routine and try to make sure that I visit the toning tables twice a week, three times whenever possible. This is not luxury but necessity.

Having seen consultants in both rheumatology and orthopaedics, I feel that the rheumatology route, rather than the orthopaedic route, is the correct medical route to follow if a person is suffering from a repetitive strain injury, as it is the soft muscle tissue that is affected.

I find many of the complimentary medicines to be of great help. Nowadays - and who knows, have I come across a cure? - I have found a fantastic acupuncturist who is working to try and release my injury. There may be a release in sight!

Life

Financial

Financially tenosynovitis took its toll. Not only did I lose a monthly income but pursuing a compensation claim meant crippling legal aid payments as well.

I attended numerous medicals, seeing 12 different specialists, in order to either claim benefits such as Disability Living Allowance and Industrial Injuries Disablement Benefit or to pursue my legal case.

After 5 years I received an out of court settlement from my employer. This does not in any way compensate for my loss. My settlement was a ¼ of my full loss of earnings up until I am 65. As I am still not able to work full time, needing regular periods of rest, it may be difficult for me to ever recoup lost earnings.

Life

Professional

At the time of my diagnosis I was working 18 hours per week as Adult Student Co-ordinator, and approximately 14 hours per week as a Swimming Teacher. Although I was on sick leave from my job as Adult Student Co-ordinator, I was able to carry on as a Swimming Teacher. That helped to keep me sane. There are aspects of my job as a Swimming Teacher where I have to ask for help. This fortunately was, and still is, always forthcoming.

It is very hard to try and explain to people exactly what it is that you've got, and why you've got it. People who work full-time on VDU's, knowing that I worked part-time, made comments such as, "Well, why haven't I got it?" When you want to be at work and all the medics are telling you that you cannot go, it is very, very frustrating.

Stress is often a contributory factor to a repetitive strain injury. For 4 to 5 months before being diagnosed with tenosynovitis I was being bullied by a work colleague, and the stress this caused did not help my situation. Prior to my sick leave I approached management about the bullying, to no avail. By the time I actually went on sick leave due to my tenosynovitis, management seemed to think that nothing more needed to be done about the bullying. It was important for my well being that I follow the grievance procedure. For 2 ½ years I struggled to seek redress.

Support Group

The Bradford Repetitive Strain Injury support group was well established when I was diagnosed with my disability. The group is my vital lifeline. In the beginning was support, and a safe haven where nobody questioned my RSI. I am with people who know exactly what I am going through. The warmth and kindness of many new people I have met has given me hope and firm friendships.

As the years have gone by, more people have come through the group, heightening my anger at employers who still allow workers to work in appalling conditions. Some of the people coming through the group these days are only in their 20's. Even though strict EEC Health & Safety Regulations have been in force since 1993, prevention is still not happening in the work place nor for that matter in education establishments.

These days I have an acceptance of my disability, and the group gives me a focus. It is an outlet through which to vent my anger and frustrations. I now campaign on behalf of the group to get the prevention of repetitive strain injuries in the workplace recognised.

My Life Now

It is now almost 9 years since my tenosynovitis diagnosis. It has been a long, turbulent struggle but by adapting my lifestyle, using physical aids, trusting my support network of family and friends, and knowing my limitations, I have a happy life.

Since April 2002 I have been able to resume computer work using Dragon NaturallySpeaking voice recognition software obtained from a company called VoicePower. The software, training and post-training has been very helpful.

Since using voice recognition software I have gone back to college where I have completed the British Computer Society's European Computer Driving Licence certificate.

I have also passed the RSA word processing intermediate exam that I was entered for at the time of my diagnosis, and am now enrolled on the RSA word processing advanced diploma course at Shipley College. The tutors there are wonderful and could not be more helpful. On approaching education establishments Shipley College were the only college willing to provide me with the Dragon NaturallySpeaking voice recognition software thus enabling me, without discrimination, to take the courses that I wanted. The college also give me full support with the examination board, who, after some dispute, accepted that I could sit their exams if I have my certificate endorsed to say that I used voice recognition software. Not a problem!

I still remain a part-time Swimming Teacher, and the voice recognition software enabled me to gain paid work as an Advice Worker at the Workers' Health Advice Team (WHAT) where I am also a volunteer. WHAT is a small, independent voluntary organisation, who through the Access to Work Scheme acquired the Dragon NaturallySpeaking voice recognition software for me.

But most of all for me, help has come from the unwavering support and trust of my colleague, who has always believed in me, waiting until I was ready, then giving me free rein to move forward in whatever direction my career is taking, allowing me the freedom to work on my own initiative again. I no longer have to sit and dictate while someone else does the typing for me. What a wonderful feeling!

In January 2002 I was approached by an employee of the NHS community hospitals in Bradford asking if I would like to be Patient Representative on their Essence of Care benchmarking. This is a government initiative by the Department of Health. In February 2003

I attended a conference with 2 other colleagues where we gave a tabletop PowerPoint presentation on Nutrition. I enjoy my voluntary work with the NHS. It has given me something to get my teeth into, using valuable knowledge and skills that I have, without affecting my disability. In turn furthering my own professional development.

Future

Nowadays, people are a little more accepting of repetitive strain injuries in that at least they may have heard of these conditions. When I was diagnosed almost 9 years ago nobody really knew what repetitive strain injury was, even though it has been around for many years within the factory and manual labour force.

One of the worst things about finding out that you have a repetitive strain injury caused by computer use is that nobody need have this injury. Instead of blaming the work force, Britain could adopt the Scandinavian way of thinking and treat the workplace as 'sick', rather than the worker. With computer technology as it is, manufacturers could make ergonomic equipment as standard. Writing to manufacturers asking them to make ergonomic equipment as standard could be the answer. As could getting the government to tackle the repetitive strain injury issue.

There are a number of different software systems already in existence which can be used. Ergo Sentry, for instance, which physically stops you from using the computer for a set period of time, and even gives you exercises to do in the interim. Voice recognition software has recently become a lot more usable, accurate and compatible with more office applications, making this a fantastic option. This type of software is quite specialised and worth investing in training from a specialist company to ensure that you have all the correct systems in place. There are also improvements to hardware such as ergonomic keyboards and mice.

Today, children are heavy users of VDU equipment and risk permanent painful injury using computers that are set up for adults. Both teachers and parents seem unaware of the dangers in schools and homes with relation to the ergonomic set up of their workstations. Repetitive strain injuries are a particular risk to children as their muscles and bones are still developing.

Professor Peter Buckle of the Robens Centre for Health Ergonomics at the University of Surrey says there are some measures put in place to minimise adult risk but little attention paid to students and schoolchildren. He says field research involving more than 2,000 youngsters show 36% of 11 to 14 year olds are suffering serious ongoing back pain and that children who suffer back pain at school are more likely to suffer in adult working life, therefore the current picture of children working in systems that appear to affect current and future health is a disturbing one. I personally would add that constant texting and mobile phone use pose a risk too.

Applying the principles of ergonomics at the design stage of new technological equipment for use in the classroom would minimise the risk to children. They have a right to work in a safe and healthy environment.

Employers have a duty of care. It is their responsibility to make employees feel comfortable in the work place by allowing them the freedom to speak out if they feel the need to alter their work pattern in any way.

Wherever possible I try to spread the message of repetitive strain injury prevention. The good news is - repetitive strain injury in the work place **IS** preventable. Getting ergonomics into the work place in the first instance **will** make a difference. Children of today are future employees in the work place. I would love to see them being given the chance to lead healthy fulfilling lives both personally and professionally.

Conclusion

'From Hand To Mouth' is a short chapter in my life and, although very personal to me, there are too many similar stories out there, which is why I was inspired to write mine.

As for me now - from the brink of a nervous breakdown, through my body's own intuitive healing process, I am on the right path.

And as for wanting to learn to type - I have come through. I CAN TYPE - I love it!

CONTACTS

Bradford Repetitive Strain Injury Support Group Tel: **01274 393949**   Visit our website on www.communigate.co.uk/brad/rsibradford/index.phtml or contact

Workers' Health Advice Team (WHAT)
An independent office situated in the UNISON Offices, 2nd Floor, Auburn House, Upper Piccadilly, Bradford, West Yorkshire, BD1 3NU; E-mail hazards@what-bohp.freeserve.co.uk

WHAT offer free help and advice with any health & safety workplace concerns whether they be musculoskeletal, backs, necks, arms, etc; stress; bullying; harassment; repetitive/noisy/dusty work; heavy lifting; asbestosis; or indeed any work related issue.

VoicePower
The Square, Farnley, Otley, West Yorkshire, LS21 2QG Tel: **01943 468000** or visit www.voicepower.co.uk providers of Dragon NaturallySpeaking voice recognition software and training.

Bradford Resource Centre
17-21 Chapel Street, Bradford, West Yorkshire, BD1 5DT Tel: **01274 779003**